Self Discipline Mastery

7 Effective Strategies to Overcome Negativity, Conquer Temptations, Build Willpower Muscles, and Finish What You Start

Nicholas Mayor

Table of Contents

Introduction

Mike and Paul are two friends of mine. We went to the same college together. Both were very popular. They both had a lot of friends. In fact, as far as I can remember, they pretty much achieved the same level of success in school.

Mike was naturally intelligent. He once bragged to me that he did not have to go to class and still rock an A. I didn't believe him at first but when I happened to take the same class he did, I saw what he was talking about with my own two eyes. There I was going to class session after session with Mike completely absent after the professor stopped taking roll in the first two weeks of school.

All those weeks passed by and I went to the final example and, lo and behold, Mike was there. Obviously, he just showed up after all that time just to take that test. It was a really bittersweet experience to discover that Mike got a way better grade than I did. I put in the time, I physically showed up, yet Mike still got a better grade.

Paul, on the other hand, made it a point to show up in class and he got the same grades as Mike. Fast forward to today and Paul is the CEO of a Silicon Valley company that's doing really well.

Conversely, Mike pretty much is a professional traveler. Don't let that euphemism throw you off. Mike has no job; he's been divorced at least a couple of times; and really doesn't have a dollar to his name.

I know that the stories of Mike and Paul are quite extreme but I share them with you because they highlight the importance of self-discipline.

Mike, as talented, naturally intelligent, and socially engaging as he was, simply lacked self-discipline. He did not know any limits. He did not know when to show up, when to work. He didn't care for any of those things.

Mike's number one priority was personal freedom. I get that. I really do. However, Paul also places a high premium on personal freedom, but lives a more financially secure life.

Self-discipline, not raw talent or potential, is the foundation of success. What if I told you that Paul's IQ was actually several notches lower than Mike's? Still, Paul was able to manage to get the same results as Mike.

It doesn't matter whether you are one standard deviation down in the IQ scale or a couple standard deviations down. There's a lot to be said about your willingness to work hard, make tough decisions, and commit.

I wish I could tell you that life success is like some sort of online menu. You click a button and after a few keystrokes, you get what you are looking for. Life doesn't work that way. In many cases, the biggest rewards life has to offer can only be "unlocked" after long, sustained periods of focused efforts.

This throws off a lot of people because we live in a time where we expect important and big rewards to be handed out at the door. That's right. You don't even have to try. You just have to show up. In fact, in many cases, a lot of people think that you don't even have to show up at all. You just have to exist, and the big things that life has to offer are given to you by right.

As anybody who has ever tried to achieve anything worthwhile in life knows firsthand, this is simply not the case. You don't get a reward just for showing up. You don't get a medal just for participating in the great game of life. Medals are few and far between; they are very hard to come by; and you have to put in the work.

Going Beyond Hard Work

I wish I could tell you that you only needed to work hard for you to be successful. The problem is you have to be able to work at a certain intensity level consistently for an extended period before the reward even materializes. This disqualifies a lot of people.
Let me tell you, it's very easy to find people who can put in the work, focus, and willpower in one day. In fact, I'm sure you would be able to do that given the proper motivation. That's not the issue. The issue is, are you willing and able to put in that kind of intensity over several weeks, months, if not, years?

Have you ever noticed that the highest paying jobs in society, generally speaking, require longer preparation? Compare the income of somebody doing clerical work at a back office somewhere and your run-of-the-mill doctor. There is no comparison. We're looking at maybe $40,000 a year compared to north of $150,000 a year depending on specialization. Do the same for lawyers where the average median income tends to be in the six figures.

The reason this is the case is because those people had to go through many more years of schooling and pass rigorous tests. In other words, they had to be disciplined enough to go through a long, grueling process. They had to pay a price most people are unable or are unwilling to pay. This is why there is a disparity.

I'm sure you can find a lot of exceptions but the exceptions simply just prove the rule. They really do because when you look at the majority of the people who attain great levels of financial and social success in the United States, you will see that they got there because they went through a process that took a tremendous amount of focus over an extended period.

Self-Discipline is the Cement of Success

If you were to erect a building and you found the necessary stone blocks as well as steel and other materials, you need something to put it all together. You need concrete. You need cement.

It doesn't really matter whether you have access to the right information. If you are not self-disciplined, you're going to have a tough time unleashing the full potential of the information you have access to. Even if you are born with good looks, great physical abilities, and athleticism, it still requires commitment, dedication, and long-term focus to turn potential into success.

The problem with a lot of people is that they think like my friend Mike. He was under the impression that he can coast on his natural abilities for life. It is beyond doubt that Mike is a smart fellow.

The problem is being smart is just one part of the equation. His situation is the same as a kid who has great basketball abilities at your local corner pickup basketball court. However, to go from there all the way to the NBA requires focus, commitment, dedication, and sacrifice. In other words, it requires self-discipline.

My friend Mike is struggling to this very day precisely because he thought he could sit on his potential. He thought that's all he needed.

I'm telling you, you may have all the natural skill and raw talent in your field but, unless you commit to fine-tuning, harnessing, and fully unleashing your potential through experience over an extended period, you're probably not going to achieve much success. You may be able to get lucky from time to time, but luck eventually runs out. As the old saying goes, "The harder you work, the luckier you get."

With self-discipline, you will be able to put in the work regardless of whether you woke up on the wrong side of the bed or not and whether you feel like it or not. You would be able to do what is expected of you day after day, week after week, month after a month, year after year regardless of what other people are saying.

People may not believe you. They might even actively oppose. None of that matters. How come? You found the internal strength that you need to keep pushing forward.

In this book, I'm going to teach you how to build self-discipline in a simplified way. By using these basic steps, you would be able to create a self-discipline framework for yourself that will give you the self-control you need to get the focus, willpower, and education true success requires.

This is a long and drawn-out process. This is not one of those "Add hot water" advice books. Far from it. You have to commit to the steps that I am going to share with you.

It's also important to understand that there is no such thing as a one-size-fits-all, magic-bullet solution to self-discipline. It doesn't exist today; it never existed; and it probably will continue to be elusive.

The best I can do for you is a framework. You have to tweak these steps and modify them to fit your day-to-day experience. In other words, you have to make them fit your personal situation. That's how you can make them truly yours.

If you approach these steps in those personal terms, you increase your likelihood of taking these steps to the next level so they produce optimal results in your personal journey to greater self-discipline. I wish you nothing but the best in your journey. Let's jump to Chapter 1.

Chapter 1: Learning Self Discipline -What It Is and What It Isn't?

Self-discipline is a very important life skill that enables you to do what's important right now and delay pleasure. In other words, you have the ability to do necessary work right now in anticipation of a better pay day, better recognition, or more status in the future.

Regardless of how you define reward, when you're a self-disciplined person, you put the hard work first. You have the ability to pay your dues upfront in anticipation of a larger payoff at some future point in time.

It also means self-control. This means that you know what you should be doing. You know what you should be thinking and saying. It may not be all that pleasant. There might be more pleasurable alternatives, but you stick to what you need to do.

This is especially true when it comes to appetite. You know that if you eat too much of certain types of food, certain bad things can happen to you. At the very least, you start to weigh more and eventually fatter and fatter or you can actually develop life-threatening diseases.

You know what's right for you and you have the ability to moderate your consumption. This applies to eating as well as drinking alcohol and other appetite choices.

The Power of Delaying Instant Gratification

You probably have heard the phrase "delayed instant gratification." What's the big deal about it?

If you look at the very big rewards in life whether we're talking about being at the top of the corporate food chain or becoming wealthy, powerful, or successful in any significant way, they all require your ability to delay gratification. It seems that the more you're able to delay gratification, the larger your long-term rewards become.

This is easier to understand when you compare delayed gratification to instant gratification. When you want to get your payoff or reward right here right now, chances are you're doing something that everybody else is doing. There's not much demand for what you're doing because everybody is doing it.

Accordingly, whatever value you provide with what you're doing is not going to be as high. Remember, everybody else is doing it. Its supply is abundant regardless of the demand so the price for whatever it is you bring to the table is very low.

People who could delay gratification, on the other hand, who have the presence of mind to stick through a long-term commitment, are able to do something that most people cannot do. Most people cannot pay their dues over a long, protracted period. People wish they could do that, but they can't. There are only a relatively few people who can stick to a plan of action all the way through, and that's why life tends to reward them much more handsomely.

Since there are only relatively few of those people, the societal demand goes up and the price they can charge for having to go through that long, drawn-out process is higher. It takes a lot of training to become a CEO of a Fortune 500 company.

It takes quite a bit of sacrifice to become a big-time lawyer or big-name doctor. Not only do you have to go through professional school, which is difficult enough as it is since the majority of the population don't go past college education level, you also have to rise through the ranks of your field. You have to put in several years of experience for you to get to the very top.

These are high-demand qualities. Society, in turn, gives you a higher reward. Lawyers and doctors, on average, make more money than the typical middle-class employee. Corporate CEOS, on average, make thousands, if not tens of thousands of times, more than a low-level employee.

This applies down the line. The more you are able to delay gratification and practice self-discipline, the more you will be able to reap the very best rewards society has to offer.

Why is Self-Discipline So Rare?

If you want me to boil down the reason to a one-word answer, it's actually quite simple. Most people prefer instant gratification. In fact, they prefer it so much they feel that there is no option. They would look at you like your some sort of freak if you tell them that you can delay gratification. All they know is instant gratification.

If you surround yourself with other people who are hell-bent on instant gratification, then it becomes abundantly clear that delayed gratification is a form of punishment. People would ask you, "Why are you doing that? Why are you putting in the time, effort, and energy over a long period when there are easier ways to go about doing it? Why are you are trying to do things the hard way when there is always a shortcut or easier alternative available?"

These are the questions people ask and this creates an environment around self-discipline that this is not very welcoming. Accordingly, even if people want to develop this personal trait, they are discouraged from doing so. This just goes to increase the demand for self-discipline and decrease the supply.

You know what happens next, right? That's right. The reward that society pays out for self-discipline goes through the roof.

The Truth about Self-Discipline

The truth about self-discipline is actually pretty straightforward. It is not a form of self-punishment. It is not some sort of ordeal. If anything, it is the very best gift you can give yourself.

You're giving yourself something that most people have either forgotten about or wish they had. You're giving yourself a trait that would enable you to come out on top regardless of whatever situation you find yourself in. You will be able to find the inner strength you need to keep going forward regardless of how adverse your circumstances may be.

The sad reality is that our society has trained most people to always take the easy way out. That has become the default reaction of most people. We're not training people to have a strong chin. Let me tell you, life will always try to punch you. Sometimes it lands a solid uppercut or right hook. When it connects, boy, are you going to feel it!

All of us have been knocked to the ground by one setback or another. The big difference between winners and everybody else is that winners are able to take the hit. They have strong chins.

Practicing self-discipline on a moment-by-moment or day-by-day basis enables you to develop that strong chin mentally and emotionally speaking. It doesn't matter how many people laugh at you; it doesn't matter how many people think you're crazy or you can't make it; you are able to put one foot in front of the other and pursue your dreams.

You are able to commit to a long-term goal and do whatever is necessary for however long it takes until you achieve victory. Even if the outcome of your efforts are not what you imagine them to be initially, you still have trained yourself to develop a character that other people would respect and admire.

In other words, you have positioned yourself to do better in the future. You have given yourself the raw ingredients that you need for eventual success. You may not have gotten the outcome that you desired. It turned out to be a bit less than you expected, but there will always be another opportunity because you have positioned yourself to take advantage of that opportunity.

Simply compare yourself to other people who did not give themselves that opportunity because they did not train themselves to be self-disciplined. They did not give themselves that character or that trait.

What Self-Discipline Isn't

Self-discipline is not inborn. I know you probably have heard many people say that self-discipline is just something that some people have and most people don't. This belief is actually self-defeating because it turns people away from the necessary process of having to form good decision-making habits.

Believe me, when you're just starting, it's so hard to make the right decision for the long-term when there are easier shortcuts in front of you. It's too easy to just go for the shortcut and call it a day. However, you know full well that if you pay your dues now, as unpleasant and inconvenient as it may be, big playoffs await you.

The problem with thinking that some people are just born with self-discipline and most aren't is that this thinking tricks you into not trying. You give yourself an excuse for refusing to develop the right mental habits today.

Many People Incorrectly Believe that Developing Self-Discipline is an Ordeal or is Somehow Hard

Let me tell you, a concept is only hard or seemingly impossible if you choose not to understand it fully. Anybody who truly understands what discipline is and how it ties into life success can see the big picture. Once they have this big picture view, they will not consider building self-discipline hard or excruciating.

Instead, they look at it as a necessary investment in themselves. They develop a different attitude. They snap to it. They can't wait to get started because they know that this is their price of admission to a better future.

Self-discipline does not make your life hard. Lack of self-discipline does. Know the difference.

When you look at self-discipline less as an ordeal because you're not doing what you'd rather but rather as a character-strengthening exercise, you develop a better attitude. You look at it on a more positive way and things become more possible.

It all boils down to the initial attitude that you have because your initial definitions and your initial perspective color what you assume and what you expect out of anything you do or any situation you find yourself in.

Don't let the different experience that you get when you are trying to build self-discipline automatically become something negative. Don't interpret it as negative. Don't interpret it as something you'd rather avoid.

Instead, adjust yourself to it. You know that you're going to have to put in the time. You know that you're going to have to figure things out as you pay your dues and work your way from the basement of that corporate ladder. That's how it works.

View what you're doing in context. Say to yourself: People who have reached the top began where you are at. Look at it as a journey.

Tap the Power of Your Neural Pathways

Self-discipline may be difficult for a lot of people because they have let their assumptions get the better of them. When they do what they're supposed to do, they look at it as something that they'd rather not do. They fill in the activity with all sorts of negative impressions and they make things all that much harder on themselves.

The good news is you can tap the power of your mind to create positive neural pathways. Did you know that if you remember something and associate a positive emotion to it, you're more likely to do it? Most importantly that neural pathway becomes more set in your mind.

It becomes habitual up to a certain point because there's no sense of emotional intimidation. You feel that what you're about to do is at least emotionally neutral. You're not scared off. You're not looking for an easy excuse. You're k not looking for a shortcut. You're not playing any of the regular games you play when you're trying to get out of a tough situation.

You let go of all of that and you jump in and do what you need to do. If you repeat this several times, the neural pathways is reset and it becomes harder and harder for you to stop. It becomes part of you and all that sense of unease or any kind of negativity simply go away.

In fact, acting on the tough decisions or tough actions that you need to make on a day-to-day basis becomes quite automatic.

Self-Discipline Does Not Have to be Drained of Emotion

A lot of people think that self-discipline simply involves raw willpower. You have this set of tasks in front of you or these set of decisions in front of you and you just have to power through.

There's no passion in it. There is no excitement about it. There's nothing to be happy about. You just have to go through it because, after all, it is an ordeal.

If you look at self-discipline in its proper context, then you can understand that it's really all about you asserting ownership over the kind of life you want to make for yourself. That's the bottom line. In other words, it's all about you taking responsibility for yourself. You realize that when you practice self-discipline, you are allowing yourself to choose your own future and your outcomes regardless of your circumstances.

It doesn't matter what other people are saying. It doesn't matter whether people are running around like chickens with their heads cut off. It doesn't matter if people are pointing at you and laughing. It doesn't matter if they're saying that it can't be done. You just make it happen.

This is the most empowering feeling in the world because you are putting in the time, effort, focus, and energy to do something that most other people would shy away from. Most other people would run for the exits and there you are pushing straight ahead to a reward they wish they can get.

If anything, this is very inspiring. Think about somebody who went against the odds. Think about somebody who beat the odds. Think about somebody who overcame despite what everybody else thought.

Far from being an emotion-free experience, self-discipline is packed with the right emotions. If you're looking for the emotional purpose, grit, a sense of overcoming, a sense of power, intensity and vindication of your dreams, this is it.

A lot of people are under the impression that self-discipline is either emotionless or reeks of negative emotions. This is due primarily to faulty assumption regarding the nature of self-discipline. They think that it is self-denial.

You're not denying yourself if you think about it. Instead, you're choosing to build the very best version of yourself. What you're denying is the part of you who runs away from responsibility. What you're denying is the person who would stay within the neat little confines of his or her comfort zone. What you're denying is the scared person who is unafraid to live up to his or her fullest potential.

You're right to deny that person and absolutely correct to focus your energy on the champion that you are inside.

There's Nothing Boring about Self-Discipline

A lot of people are under the impression that when you practice self-discipline, you're basically just doing the same thing over and over again. You think of having to eat salads instead of German chocolate cake, having to go to the gym and lift weights instead of just going to the corner bar and drinking with your buddies. You think about following the law while instead of having a great time with your friends causing a lot of mayhem.

The truth is self-discipline unlocks a far more exciting world than the kind of world you're stuck with if you have absolutely no self-discipline. Let me tell you, if you have absolutely no self-discipline, you'll be stuck in the middle. You're going to be unhappy with your income. You're going to be constantly comparing yourself to other more successful people. You would always jealous of what other people had and say all sorts of justifications to yourself why they have things that you cannot afford.

People think that this is exciting but this is really boring. It's all too predictable. In fact, there's nothing exciting or sexy about feeling stuck, frustrated, and left behind. Those are precisely the kinds of sentiments you would be feeling if you do not choose to practice self-discipline.

Make no mistake, there's nothing boring about investing in the kind of future life or future outcome you desire for yourself and your family. In fact, with the right self-discipline, you access the most non-boring feeling in the world.

What feeling is that? Freedom. When you have freedom, there's hope. When you have hope, there is possibility. Life is an adventure. Everything is wide open because you have the skills, talent, and, most importantly, resources to do what you want to do, when you want to do it, however you want to do it.

You can't say the same when you are stuck in a dead-end job, in a dead-end existence in the middle of nowhere because you chose to do the quick and easy instead of the hard and necessary.

The good news is you can choose to overcome these misconceptions about self-discipline and get on the right path right here, right now.

Chapter 2: 12 Reasons Why People Have A Tough Time Developing Self Discipline

There is no "one size fits all" reason why people struggle with self-discipline. Still, if you were going to boil down these many different reasons, you probably would come up with the following list. Again, this is a generalized list. Your particular personal reason may be different. Still, the list below pretty much covers the vast majority of people's difficulties with developing self-discipline.

Reason #1

A lot of people think that developing self-discipline is hard and is a form of self-denial.

If you define yourself as somebody who easily goes for something more pleasurable rather than doing something necessary and hard, you'd have a tough time with self-discipline. However, you don't have to define yourself that way. If you define yourself that way, you would think that you're denying yourself when you choose to go the other way, which is of course to be more self-disciplined.

To fix this problem, just change your definition of self-discipline. Assume that it isn't hard. Assume that it is some sort of investment in yourself.

Reason #2

We surround ourselves with people who are absolutely not disciplined.

It is hard to soar like an eagle when you are surrounded by turkeys or chickens. This is absolutely true. If all the people you surround yourself with, or who you look up to have absolutely no self-discipline, then it is going to be very hard.

What is the solution? Find new friends. Birds of a feather flock together. If you'd like to develop new values, hang out with people who have those values. It's as simple as that. You plug yourself into a social network that reinforces certain shared values.

Reason #3

We are scared stiff of failure

Let me tell you, fear is a very strong emotion. I'm sure you already know that. However, the problem is if you are not developing self-discipline, you are already setting yourself up for failure. Whatever it is you fear about failure is going to happen, and you are going to make it happen. The solution to this, of course, is to do something different from what you're doing now.

In other words, choose to be more self-discipline if you are afraid of failure. The more self-disciplined you are, the stronger you become, and the less likely you will fail.

Reason #4

We feel we don't have a strong inner core of persistence and effort

If you don't have a track record of committing to a goal and sticking to it, regardless of the difficulties and discouragement you encounter, it doesn't mean that it's the end of the world, seriously. What this means is that you're going to have to put one foot in front of the other and try.

Building self-discipline is one of those things that you master as you do it. It is not something that you master by simply thinking about it, or coming up with some sort of emotional or intellectual catharsis. It doesn't work that way.

For you to be self-disciplined, you have to do it. And worse yet, for many people, it's something that you have to do day after day. The good news is the more you do it, the easier it becomes.

Reason #5

Laziness pays off now

I know, I know; laziness has an instant payoff. You don't need to convince me of this. After all, before I discovered the steps that I write about in this book, I considered myself lazy. I would always look for the most painless and effortless "solution" to my issue.

The problem is anything worthwhile in life requires discomfort. You're going to have to step out of your comfort so you're going to have to sacrifice. You're going to have to overcome. That's why they are worthwhile, and the things that we easily do, most people can do.

That's why they are low-value activities. Just look at the value you place on yourself and ask yourself, "Is being lazy worth the sacrifice I am making?" You're sacrificing a lot just to remain lazy, believe it or not. You're sacrificing a great future. You're sacrificing a higher-value character. You're letting all of that go for chump change that you get now.

Reason #6

We are easily distracted

A lot of people think that self-discipline is simply impossible because they just have short attention spans. They get easily distracted, they can't stick to a path. They can't focus on what they need to do. This doesn't have to be the case.

You're distracted easily because that's all you know. Maybe now is the time to unwind that and come up with something better. Just because you are easily distracted now doesn't mean that you're going to continue to be easily distracted forever.

You can make it change now. You can focus on things that require a tremendous amount of attention to detail and long-term focus. You can make that decision right here, right now. There's nothing stopping you from that. If anything, whatever problems you may have about lacking focus and possessing only a ridiculously short attention span, can be solved by this new decision that you're to make.

Reason #7

Going for the quick payoff weakens self-discipline

It's very easy to develop a habit of going for the quick payoff. It's very easy to just take the path of least resistance time and time again. In fact, this can become almost automatic. When you are given any kind of choice, you automatically make the "easiest choice."

Well, since you already know that taking the easy way out reduces your self-discipline, or prevents you from becoming more self-disciplined, you have enough information. What am I talking about? Well, you know the link between doing what you normally do and your lack of self-discipline. You also should know what you are missing out on when you don't have self-discipline.

Now, put all these together, and you would quickly see a direct link from instinctively going for the quick and easy shortcut, compared to putting in the hard work and committing to the necessary sacrifices so you can achieve greater results. You know how everything fits. The only question is, are you willing to do something about it?

Reason #8

People avoid being self-disciplined because they have low self-esteem

Low self-confidence, and low self-esteem go hand in hand. If you don't have a high opinion of yourself, your ability to get things done, what you're capable of, and who you are, nobody should be surprised why you don't trust your ability to get things done. They do flow from each other.

The good news is this doesn't have to continue. When you do things that are hard and necessary now, you build competence. You start making progress in certain areas of your life. Those can improve the way you look at yourself.

It turns out that if you're able to do these, you're not as big of a loser as you think you are. Your self-esteem improves as you become more and more competent. As you see more and more positive outcomes in your life, you start feeling better about yourself and your capabilities, and this enables you to become more confident.

You're more likely to keep going forward, and putting in the necessary effort, and making the right sacrifices until you eventually achieve bigger and bigger results. Lack of self-esteem should not block you from developing self-discipline. If anything, self-discipline, or at least the pursuit of it, is the solution to low self-esteem.

Reason #9

We can't set a goal even if our lives depended on it

If you don't have a goal, or you think you already have goals, but you're basically just chasing your tail, listen up. Just because you don't have a direction doesn't mean you have to continue that way. You just need to sit down and ask yourself what kind of life you would like for yourself.

How much how much assets would you like to have? Would you like to travel? Would you like some sort of financial freedom? Would you like to be able to do whatever you want? Well, if you can imagine that, then you have the initial outline of a life goal. What you're looking for is freedom.

Sadly, freedom is not free; it is earned by hard work. If you're looking for any kind of financial freedom, you have to lay the right foundations. You have to make the right sacrifices. You have to build the right things, and this requires goal-setting. And goals are actually easier than you think.

In fact, people set goals all the time. The problem is they frame them in the form of fantasies. They imagine them, just so they can get this emotional release from the day-to-day drudgery of their lives. This is really too bad because if you're able to set goals, you will be able to start working on them.

That's how you become a more effective person. When you set a goal, and you put in the work, focus, and effort to make those goals happen, you become a better person. How come? Well, just compare yourself to other people.

People are not shy when it comes to fantasizing and talking about grandiose dreams, hopes and "goals." But when the time comes for the rubber to meet the road, nothing. Everybody talks a good game, but they cannot walk their talk. Be that person who actually sets a goal and does everything he or she can to make those goals happen.

That's how you build self-discipline, and that's also how you build a better life for yourself; these go hand-in-hand. Just because you don't have a goal right now, or it's very fuzzy, is no excuse.

Reason #10

Procrastination has become a habit

Did you know that building self-discipline is the antidote to procrastination? Let me tell you, most of the people I know, who have serious problems with procrastination, know that procrastination is a bad thing. In fact, a lot of them treat it like a big monkey on their back.

They'd love to get it off. They'd love to be free of procrastination. They know how bad it is. In many cases, it has cheated them of their lives's big goals. They know that, but they are so scared of self-discipline, and imagine it to be something that it's not, that they can't beat the procrastination habit.

The good news is self-discipline is the way to beat procrastination. If you allow yourself to do one thing every single day, no matter how small it is, you're one step closer to beating procrastination once and for all. Once you're able to do one thing for a particular day, then scale it up to two things. And then, before you know it, you're able to do a lot of things.

These are things that you'd normally put off. These are things that you would normally duck out of. When you're able to knock them out, because you have set your mind to do them and committed to them regardless of how you're feeling and regardless of what other people are doing around you, you have become self-disciplined.

Interestingly enough, that's precisely the point in time where you've also destroyed procrastination. These go hand-in-hand. ==Don't let your fear of self-discipline keep you from beating procrastination.==

Reason #11

Lack of ambition, motivation, or willpower

You have to understand that if you are able to dream of a better life for yourself, you are able to visualize an alternative reality that can act as a map out of the life of desperation, frustration, or inertia you're in. ==You won't be reading this book if you are 100% happy with your life, okay, let's not kid ourselves.==

You know the areas for improvement in your life. This is why it's really important to understand that if you are able to visualize a better life for yourself, that is a good enough place to start with, seriously. List it down, get excited about them, reduce them to specific outcomes that are realistic and attainable.

Now that you have converted your fantasy or daydream into something more realistic, you can then break down the goals or sub-goals that would help those outcomes become a reality. Once you are able to get those goals down, you can then reduce them into daily tasks. What do you do with these daily tasks? Well, you can reduce them further into a single task every day.

Now, ask yourself "Can I do this task? Will I allow myself to do this? Do I give myself permission to do this?" If you're able to do that, pat yourself on the back. You're one step closer to your life goal. Dream big, but break it down into a million tiny pieces, and you'd be surprised as to the power of your commitment to that one piece which leads to another piece, which leads to another. And if you are able to scale this up and allow your passion and your sense of pride to kick in, you will be able to go all the way.

Be proud of the fact that you can dream. Be proud of the fact that you are able to knock out even one tiny sliver of the actions needed to make that dream a reality. Because is if you're able to do one, you can do two. If you're able to do two, eventually you will get to three. Do you know where I'm coming from?

The worst thing that you can do is to play this game with yourself and say, "Well, I just don't have any ambition" or "Motivation just escapes me." You're just playing games with yourself. You're just giving yourself an excuse not to start.

Everybody can daydream. Everybody can fantasize about a better life for themselves. Start with those, and if you break them down enough, and you spread them evenly enough, where you start with something that is so easy to do, like make a phone call, look something up on the Internet, and then on to the next step the next day, eventually, it will scale up.

Eventually, the successes that you are able to achieve in the past start compounding. They start building up on top of each other, and before you know it, you would have achieved your goal. The best part to all of this? You have also developed self-confidence and self-discipline along the way.

Reason #12

Some people are just born with self-discipline

This is the worst reason that you can give yourself, really. It's an excuse. So what, some people are born with a tremendous amount of self-discipline? They don't take anything away from you, there is enough self-discipline to go around.

The problem is most people are running away from it. Most people don't even want to develop it in the first place. Stop the thinking that just because you weren't born with self-discipline, that there is no hope for you. Most self-discipline is a learned trait. Get that through your head.

It is not something that just dropped on somebody's lap. It's not something that they stumbled upon. It's something that they actually worked on. It's something that they chose to develop. If other people can develop it, what's stopping you?

Stop giving in to excuses, because thinking that self-discipline is somehow inborn is exactly that, it's an excuse. Stop robbing yourself of the victory you could otherwise be enjoying.

Chapter 3: 7 Most Effective Strategies on How To Self Discipline

Now, this is an overview chapter. I'm going to give you a quick rundown of the seven techniques for building self-discipline in a simple, yet effective way. Again, as I have mentioned in the introduction of this book, these seven steps are to function as a starting framework. You have to treat it as a starting point.

As you implement each of the steps, you should fine-tune them to fit your particular set of circumstances. With enough modification, you can scale up their effect, and they will be able to help you become increasingly self-disciplined, as you make progress with each succeeding step. The whole point here is to create a compounding, self-sustaining system that eventually becomes automatic.

That's right. It becomes a habit, but that's not going to happen if you do not fine-tune each of the steps, so it makes perfect sense in your particular situation. Everybody's different, everybody has different experiences. Everybody is doing different things and has different lives. You can't expect some sort of one-size-fits-all magic bullet solution.

The best you can do is to take these seven techniques and tweak them around the particular details of your life. I can't emphasize this enough, because this is the secret to fully unlocking the effectiveness and tremendous success you could get with these seven techniques. Without further ado, here are the seven techniques.

Minimize distractions and overcome temptations

Your first step is to cut down on activities, thought patterns, and everything else that throw you off track. When you minimize distractions, overcoming temptations becomes easier, because you have the proper emotional and mental resources you need to overcome temptations when you have adequately freed up your resources.

Develop a plan of action and commit

Anybody can plan, but relatively few people can commit. Know the difference; commitment is not just some sort of verbal proclamation. It is not just agreeing to something. Instead, it's something that you actually do on a day-to-day basis over a long period of time.

Create a backup plan when self-discipline starts to dwindle

The worst thing that you can do is to work on building up your self-discipline with the expectation that everything will go smoothly once you start. Most people fail to build up self-discipline because they think that becoming self-disciplined from where they were was a simple case of going from point A to point B. You have to be adequately, mentally, and emotionally prepared for the times when your self-discipline is challenged, or is in short supply. A little bit of preparation goes a long way.

Regularly flex your willpower muscles

Self-discipline runs on willpower. Willpower, it turns out, is just like a physical muscle set.

When you go to the gym, and you work on your muscle sets and put pressure on them, they become stronger. You also become leaner and more powerful, and the same applies to your willpower. The key is to regularly challenge and put pressure on your willpower.

Take care of yourself through exercise or meditation, adequate sleep, and a healthy diet

Self-discipline does not exist in a vacuum. It must have a firm foundation of good health, the right mental state, and a sense of mindfulness. Thankfully, these are things that you can easily work on.

Overcome personal negativity

It's very easy to look at what you're doing from a very negative perspective. In fact, it's very easy to think you're just wasting your time. After all, if you felt that you have been unsuccessful in the past, what makes this situation any different? You have to overcome your negativity because otherwise, it's going to swallow up your efforts at building self-discipline. It doesn't matter how excited you are when you began. It doesn't matter how pumped up you are, all of that will go straight down the toilet if you allow your negativity to take over.

A little bit of belief goes a long way

If you believe that you can be self-disciplined, you are positioning yourself for success. A little bit of belief in yourself is crucial not to make things happen. Unfortunately, if you go into this with doubting that you can pull it off, or if you have the right mental and emotional resources to make it happen, you may be sabotaging yourself. You may be stepping into a self-fulfilling prophecy that can lead to negativity, disappointment, and an ever decreasing opinion of what you're capable of; not a good move.

Now that you have a good overview of the seven techniques that I'm going to step you through, I'm going to go ahead and drill down into each of these techniques. Please know that these techniques are backed by actual behavioral science research. This is not just my opinion, there is actual hard science to back up the claims behind these techniques. You have to master each of these techniques.

The good news is you can start with the beginning, and then scale up over time. You're in no rush. What's important is to just keep at it until you have mastered it.

Chapter 4: Minimize Distractions to Control Impulses & Resist Temptations

The first thing you need to do is to simplify how you do things. Do you go through some sort of elaborate ritual? Obviously, that ritual is not paying off. Do you go through some sort of mental steps? Obviously, there's a lot to be desired as far as how you think about the things you should be doing. Try to simplify how you're doing things.

Do you have to go to the bathroom first before you sit down to work? Do you do some sort of elaborate ritual, like cleaning out your desk, or rearranging stuff before you get down to work? Maybe these are just distracting you. Maybe they are eating up precious willpower instead of you pushing yourself to get things done in as little time possible. The better approach would be to minimize all distractions. This means turning off your mobile devices for the time being. This means refusing to check email for a fixed period of time.

Step up gradually

The good news is that you don't have to carry out all these recommendations all at once. You can take baby steps. You can choose to do one small thing at a time. You don't have to do everything at once. At first, you may want to clear up your desk, and then see if that improves your willingness to get started with work.

Next, you may want to shut down all devices, and see if that it lengthens the time at which you can work intensively. What's important is that you are tracking your progress. In the beginning, you may be able to only go a full 10 minutes of straight, clean, pure work, and that's okay. You might be thinking that 10 minutes is too short of the time. Well, don't worry, don't beat yourself up. You made it to 10 minutes.

The next day, try to make it to 11 minutes, and then 12 minutes after that. Maybe you're feeling really good the next day and try to bump it up to 15. However, way you want to do this, as long as you're making incremental progress, and most importantly, you're not backtracking or backsliding; you are doing well. This means that if you can get from 10 to 11, then to 13, then to 15, without ever going back, you're doing well.

Sometimes, it may feel and seem like you're stuck, but that's okay. As long as you're not going back, you're fine. As long as your attention span is not decreasing, and your actual work time is moving forward regardless of how slow, you're doing well.

The power of clearing distractions to remove temptation

In a 2006 study out of Cornell University, published in the international Journal of Obesity, 40 subjects were studied. They were given work areas. The researchers placed certain containers near the work areas. The test participants were given a choice of either putting chocolate candy and in a hidden desk drawer, or putting it in one of the containers approximately 2 meters away from them which they can see.

These containers were opaque or clear. Each container was refilled with candy at the end of each day, at around evening time. The amount of chocolates consumed by the participants were recorded, was followed up by a series of questionnaires, and then analyzed.

The study showed that the participants who routinely hid their candy are less likely to eat them, compared to the participants who kept their candy it in a container that is in plain sight. It didn't matter whether the container was opaque or see-through, their chocolate consumption levels were much higher than the participants who hid their chocolate.

This shows that if the distraction is out of sight, it is also out of mind. You are more likely to overcome your temptation to that item if it is not available. It doesn't matter whether that temptation takes the form of email or social media updates. As long as you make it inaccessible, It is out of mind and you're more likely to focus.

Similarly, in another study, published in of 2016 by Cornell University involving snacking habits, researchers found that the layout of particular offices might lead to excessive snacking. Just by placing the beverage station in the office kitchen closer to the snack bar, researchers showed that proximity to tempting snacks played a big role in the amount of snacks employees at Google's New York office enjoyed over an extended period of time.

In fact, when the beverage station was positioned closer to snacks, office workers were 69% more likely to snack than when the beverage unit was placed farther away. The bottom line is by taking what would normally tempt you out of commission, or removing it from sight, you make things easier on yourself. Of course, this is not a slam dunk. This is not some sort of magic bullet, but it definitely helps you get a headstart.

The key is to open up a "productivity gateway" when previously, none existed. You're reading this book because you're struggling with self-discipline, and chances are you probably can't even go a pure one hour of hard work. The good news is you don't have to start with one hour of pure unadulterated work.

You can start with 10 minutes, and then keep increasing that gateway period because you have overcome temptations by clearing distractions and removing access to the things that would normally distract you or take away attention from your task at hand.

Chapter 5: Develop A Clear Plan of Action, Be Decisive and Commit Fully

If you want to develop self-discipline, first, be clear about what you want to be disciplined about. This is crucial; you can't just look at self-discipline like a morphous idea or concept that you're just going to run after, that's not going to work. It's too vague, it's too ambiguous. Chances are you might end up running around in circles because you're not really sure what you're trying to accomplish.

You have to be as clear as possible as to what exactly you're trying to be disciplined about. At work, what is it that you're normally struggling with? I'm sure you're not struggling across the board. I'm sure that when it comes time for you to go to a meeting, like most people, you don't have a problem with that.

So, if your boss says, "Hey, let's go to that restaurant around the corner, it's my treat!," you probably don't have a problem with that. So it's very important to be clear about what it is about your general struggles that you are having the most difficulty with. The more specific you are, the more progress you will make.

Next, you need to create a clear outline of the steps you need to take. For example, if you are struggling with being productive at work, then the first thing you need to focus on is what type of work are you having a tough time with. And then once you have identified that, outline it. What are the steps that you need to do to handle that task? For example, if you work at an Internet marketing company, your typical online marketing task package would probably involve a mix of research, planning, implementation, outreach, monitoring, and optimization.

Those are many moving parts. Maybe you don't have a problem with outreach, but you struggle with everything else. Maybe research and planning are not a big deal to you, but when it comes to reaching out to other people via email, you get cold feet. The worst thing that you can do is to just say to yourself, "I'm having a tough time with work." That's not going to cut it because it's too broad. You have to slice and dice what you actually do in those eight hours so you can zero in on what you can a focus your self-discipline on.

It's not very efficient to try to be self-disciplined about the whole package when most of the things that you do are actually pretty straightforward to you; you don't have any issues with them. You just focus, instead, on the few components that you are struggling with.

This is how you set up a clear goal, because your goal is to focus on those sub-segments, not the whole burrito, so to speak. Indeed, psychologists have noticed that people are more effective when they focus on a single, or really simplified goal instead of trying to take on a whole package of goals at once. The same applies to your work, your school, your relationships, your issues at the gym.

Zero in on what you're actually struggling with in terms of self-discipline, and prioritize those. Those should be your goals. Your goal is to do a much better job with a specific task, or small set of tasks, and you have to hold yourself to account by setting up a set of expected results. You can just fool yourself into thinking that you're making progress by saying, "I just want to get better at X." That's not going to cut it.

Indeed, in a study released by the Journal of Consumer Research a few years back, researchers discovered that study participants who try to accomplish several goals at once were not very likely to succeed. They could not commit fully, and are less likely to produce the desired outcome compared to people who were just assigned a single goal. People packing several goals at once were distracted and couldn't do a uniformly good job compared to people who just had one task.

The study was set up among MBA students and business school staffers. The participants were split up into two groups. Some participants were given a to-do list that contained six goals, others just had one goal. Goals varied quite a bit from eating a very healthy meal to reading a book for pleasure, or calling someone they haven't talked to in a while.

As you can tell, these tasks were pretty simple and straightforward. After observing, the participants were then asked to report whether they actually carried out their task list. It turns out that those who were only assigned one single target goal were able to finish, compared to those with those with a lot more goals.

The key here is to plan out what you're going to do on a task-by-task basis. Obviously, you should put higher priority tasks first; these are the ones that have a higher payoff value. Maybe you should do the 80/20 or Pareto principle analysis on your daily tasks. Indeed, of all the tasks that you do in any given day, only 20% actually account for 80% of your results.

Chapter 6: A Solid Contingency Plan When Self Discipline Starts Waning

Let's get one thing clear, it is very easy to assume that you are going to have a straight shot at self discipline. In fact, it is tempting to look at building self discipline as yet another life project. If you look at your other life projects like going on a diet, finding better job and getting promoted more often; if you're like most people a common thread arises.

If you are pretty much like everybody else you probably would assume that once you get started, everything will proceed smoothly. A lot of people think this way and that is why when they encounter some turbulence with their plans, they fold quickly like a folding chair. It Is pretty sad, but it is entirely avoidable.

You have to understand that you have to intend your implementation of your goal. According to psychologist Peter Gollwitzel, in a paper published in 1999, if you want to increase the likelihood of your goals, becoming reality, you have to have a high level of implementation intention. In other words you have to look at your goals not so much as a finished spate of reality that takes place sometime in the future but as a series of statements. These are not just regular statements like you will go somewhere, achieve something, earn a certain amount of money or be with certain traits or qualities.

Instead Gollwitzel said that a high intention plan is a series of "if-then" statements. This enables you to overcome whatever complications, curve balls or unforeseen circumstances, you may encounter in the future. By intending your implementation through a preset series of contingency plans, you increase the likelihood of getting to where you want to go.

For example, if you want to earn a million dollars a year in ten years you may want to have an intention implementation plan that covers the most common contingency. If you run out of capital you go to A, B and C. If this opportunity path doesn't pan out you are going to look at A, B and C. If your business partner for whatever reason decides to check out you will check out X, Y and Z.

Implementation plans made up of "if-then" statements enable you to fully map out the range of most likely possibilities in front of you. There is a lower likelihood of nasty surprises. Please understand that people who achieve success through consistent effort are not necessarily smarter than everybody else. Instead, they are able to stick through their plan and put in the very best they have got for however long it takes because they have these "if-then" statements in mind.

 They are not caught flat footed. They are not like the proverbial deer caught in headlamps and headlights. They know how to scramble, they know how to hustle when the stuff hits the fan.

Unfortunately, I can't say the same for a lot of people trying to become more self disciplined. If for whatever reason things don't pan out the way they had hoped, they quickly fold. They give up. They get confused, they get frustrated and eventually they give up.

The last time I checked, the only time you can fail is when you give up. Too many people give up too quickly when they could otherwise have developed a very high level of self discipline.

It Is Important To Hold Some Of Your Wheel Power In Reserve As Part Of Your   contingency   Plan

Your first step should be to have a backup plan when thinks go south, as far as your self discipline journey goes. Parallel to this, you should also have a way of tapping your reserve will power. If you are properly motivated you will be able to tap into these deep reserves of will power. This is very important because a lot of people think that they only have so much of will power in any given day and for the most part this is true as far as appearances are concerned.

As far as your conscious awareness goes, you only have so much will power to spare in any given day. However, people have been shown through psychology experiments to possess deep reserves of will power. These are will power reserves that they are unaware of. You have to have the proper motivation to tap into these   reserves.

In a paper published in personality and social psychology bulletin by researchers from the university of Albany in 2003. Researchers found that when they tested 4300 graduate students using both creativity and cognitive ties, that those students who were given the impression that their testing is in conjunction with Alzheimer's disease treatment, were better. These are people whose will power were already depleted through passels, but they persisted because they thought that if they went through with the test, they may be able to help find an Alzheimer's disease cure.

The study suggests that when people operating under high levels of motivation they may be able to overcome situations where their will power is depleted or nearly so. Of coarse there are limits to this, but this is a tremendously significant study. It turns out that we have more will power than we gave ourselves credit for. The key is to be properly motivated so we can go all the way. We actually have a lot of will power in the bank than we care to realize.

Study Proves The Power Of Backup Plans

Backup plans as mentioned above can be phrased in terms of implementation intention.

You create a series of "if-then" statement when you are going through a task. As you work towards a goal you can rely on these "if-then" statements to guide you through similar response.

This concept was tested by researchers who published their results in the journal "Psychology and Health" in 2007. This study involved obese or overweight women who were part of a commercial weight reduction program. Participants were randomly assigned to either a controlled group or were given an implementation intention statement.

Those who had an implementation intention coaching lost 4.2 kg on average. The controlled group lost only half of this amount on average. This study highlights the fact that when people have some sort of "backup plan" mindset, they are more likely to succeed.

Step By Step Guide To Implementation Intention

First, you have to lay out your goal. What is it that you are trying to achieve? Next, review the steps that you already know or have already planned on doing to get to that goal. At this point you are not really looking at anything new. What makes the implementation intention system different from typical goal setting involves obstacles.

Now that you have a clear idea of your goal, how to get there and how to measure your arrival at your destination or how to measure success in terms of outcomes, the next step is to list possible challenges, probably the most probable setbacks that you may possibly encounter.

Once you have listed those, break them into if statements. Once you have done that lay out a concise answer or backup action.

When you do this you create a series of programs that you can implement automatically or nearly so that gets you out of a bind. For example, you can say to yourself if I am feeling tapped out, I will go grab a quick salad to get a nice boost of energy. Similarly, if I am feeling really stressed out, then I will take a swim or walk around the block.

By clearly laying out your backup plan and how you should respond to curve balls or unforeseen circumstances, you are laying the groundwork for eventual success. You are not caught by surprise.

Chapter 7: How to Flex and Strengthen Willpower Muscles

If you want to be a self disciplined person, please understand that you have to put some stress on your willpower. You can talk about building self discipline all you want. You may think about all the things about being more self disciplined that you have somehow discovered along the way.

This all sounds great and it definitely gives you a great emotional buzz. But let me tell you, until and unless you actually try using your willpower and putting it to the test, you're just wasting your time. Self discipline is one of those personal traits, like patience, that you only build up by using.

It's only when you get tested, tempted and challenged that you build self discipline. If you don't put any stress on it or if you stick to your comfort zone, you're not building self discipline. The only person you're fooling is yourself.

You have to put it to the test. It doesn't have to be big. It doesn't have to be overly dramatic. It doesn't have to be grandiose. As long as you use it day after day, moment after moment, it gets stronger and stronger.

The best news? You can test it in small ways. Even low scale testing is good. As long as you're constantly testing it and then subjecting it to really big tests of will, then you will make progress.

Self discipline is not an inborn trait. Some people might seem like they were born with it. But it's a learned behavior. It's a skill that you pick up from your many years of living. It only arises in a fully meaningful way when you are actually confronted with situations that requires self discipline.

I'm not just talking about getting tested from time to time. I'm talking about getting tested day after day after day. That's how you make progress. It's all about daily practice. The good news is if you know the right way to go and you choose that path one day, it gets easier and easier.

In fact, the more you choose it, the easier it becomes. You establish a sense of momentum. It starts scaling in on itself and it becomes part of you. But the problem is you will never get to that point of repetition if you don't start.

Building willpower and discipline is like building muscles when you exercise. If you've ever done any weight training at the gym, you know that it can be murder on your muscles. The first time you put a significant amount of stress on your muscle structures, it hurts like hell the next day or the day after that.

This is the point where a lot of people are tempted to just quit going to the gym. They are feeling sore, they feel that this is more trouble than its worth and they give themselves all sorts of excuses and justifications why they should stop.

But if you find the will to keep going to the gym and applying pressure to your muscles and stressing them properly despite the pain, what do you think happens? Seemingly like magic, all that pain disappears overnight because you have retrained your muscle mass.

It's as if your muscles know that you're not going anywhere. You're going to be putting in the work day after day so your muscle aches and pains quickly go away and you start making serious progress. The same process applies to your willpower.

It's very easy to just quit. It's very easy to just throw in the towel because it seemed like you got in over your head. For whatever reason, every time you step up to a certain situation, you end up making the wrong call.

The good news is once you make that right decision and you stick to it day after day or situation after situation, it gets easier and easier. At the back of your head, you know that since you've done this before, you can do it again and again and again.

In a Case Western Reserve University study released in 1999 published in the journal of social psychology, 69 college students spend a couple of weeks doing one of several self control exercises. These involve monitoring and documenting what they ate, regulating their mood or improving their posture.

People who went through self control stress exercises perform better in terms of resistance to willpower depletion compared to students who did not go through those self control exercises. Please understand that those exercises added stress to their willpower.

But it turns out that added stress actually strengthened their willpower and guarded against rapid willpower depletion. Similarly in a 2010 study published in the journal of experimental social psychology, 92 test participants were randomly assigned 4 tasks for a couple of weeks.

They're to keep a diary, do some math problems, avoid sweets and improve their hand grip. These people were given different directions. For people who were told to avoid sweets, they were instructed to avoid as much dessert foods like candy, pies, cookies and cake.

It turns out that people who were instructed to do little acts of self control performed better overall. Since they were asked to resist small temptations along the way, this scaled up and built up over time and they are able to inhibit their normal responses.

This study suggests that if you stress your willpower muscles, even incrementally, you can scale up your results. You'd be surprised as to how much self control you are actually capable of.

Chapter 8: Daily Simple Practices to Make You More Self Disciplined

When you build up a proper foundation for your mental state as well as your physical health, you create a platform for better self control. Please understand that this long perceived division between mind and body is actually non-existent.

In fact, several studies show that when you are in bad physical shape, your risk of developing mental and emotional health issues increase. It also works the other way around. If you're feeling stressed all the time or you're depressed or your mental health is in bad shape, this can have a corrosive effect on your overall physical health.

Your mental and emotional state can actually leave you at higher risk of developing some medical conditions. By the same token, if you don't get enough sleep, this can have a very strong effect on your self control.

Sleep deprivation can be a serious problem as far as mood regulation and your general mental state and, of course, your physical health. If you fail to eat regularly, this can create a cascading effect that impacts your mental, emotional and physical health.

This is why it's really a good idea to monitor blood sugar levels because blood sugar is usually the only fuel your brain uses. If you have massive spikes in your blood sugar, this can have a tremendous effect on both your mental and physical health.

In a 2009 study done by the university of Exeter which was eventually published in the medical journey appetite, researchers looked at the effect of brisk everyday walking on subject's urge to eat chocolate. They also measured the subject's physiological and psychological responses to stress.

The study involved 25 people who ate chocolate regularly. After they have stopped eating chocolate completely for 3 days, they were randomly assigned into 2 groups. One group was to take a 15 minute brisk walk, which is semi self paced. The rest were not asked to take a 15 minute brisk walk.

The participants blood pressure were then measured in terms of their response to the temptation of holding a chocolate bar. This was the researcher's way of determining cravings.

It turned out that the test participants who were asked to walk on a treadmill at a slow pace for 15 minutes were actually less likely to crave the chocolate compared to the control group. Surprisingly, the brisk walkers also had lower blood pressure.

In a study released by Clemson University published in 2015 in the journal Frontiers in Human Neuro Science, people who were not getting enough sleep due to chronic insomnia suffered impaired self control when tested.

This study suggests that when people don't get enough sleep on a consistent basis, they are more likely to be distracted and make impulsive decisions.

Step by step solution

It's a good idea to get plenty of regular exercise. Also, adjust your sleeping schedule so you get a full 8 hours of sleep. It's also a good idea to practice mindfulness yoga or meditation. Adopt some sort of practice that would set your mind at ease.

You should also eat healthier by eating a very balanced meal everyday. This way, you create a healthier personal platform in which self control and self discipline can thrive. Without a firm foundation made possible by better mental, emotional and physical health, you're just making things harder on yourself when you try to build up self control.

The things that you go through might actually add more stress to your system. Your system might not be able to handle such extra stress on a consistent basis.

Chapter 9: Step-by-Step Process To Conquer Negativity

I'm not asking you to become a completely different person. After all, we all have different personalities. It doesn't make any sense to adopt some sort of homogeneous personality or personal profile.

Still, in research study after researcher study, negative thinking can get in the way of you leading a productive life. If you want to develop high levels of self control, you can't get the outcome you're looking for if you're riddled with doubt, unnecessary skepticism or are overly negative.

I'm not saying that there's absolutely no space for skepticism or looking at the negative side in your life. In many situations, a little bit of healthy skepticism is more than welcome. The problem is when you are overly negative, you destroy your chances of success because the name of the game is to do something you would rather not do over an extended period of time.

In other words, you have to have willpower stamina. The problem with negativity is it just pushes you closer and closer to frustration and, eventually, giving up. If you think that what you're doing is a complete and total waste of time, it's very easy for you to get frustrated.

After you are frustrated several times, it becomes very easy for you to just assume that what you're doing is completely pointless and it's time for you to quit. All it takes to reverse this sad progression is a little bit of optimism.

When you are optimistic about the outcome or you're positive that somehow, someway, things will fall into place and you'll be okay, you're more likely to stick to it. You have to understand that self discipline is not a "one time big time" experience. It's never been.

This is one of those personal traits that you have to work on for a lifetime. It's all about your lived experience. If you don't have the necessary level of optimism, it's very easy to just second guess yourself, sabotage yourself and fall to a long list of distractions that can lead to failure.

For example, you're working on being more self disciplined and you're sticking to a task you'd rather avoid and all of a sudden, some opportunity comes by or is presented to you. You think that this is a better deal. You think that this will lead you to a better place in your life and you drop everything.

This is called a shiny object syndrome and it is all too real. People who suffer from this syndrome jump from one project to another, one opportunity to another, one sex or romantic partner after another only to end up with nothing at the end.

I know it sounds sad. It definitely sounds tragic. But it's all too real. These individuals look over their shoulders and all they can see is a long trail of half implemented ideas, half completed projects and a lot of broken and shattered dreams and relationships.

The secret is to get rid of negativity. It's like a mental cancer that creeps into everything that you think about, talk about and attempt to do. Unless you get a handle on your negativity, it threatens to undermine and, eventually, sabotage your efforts in becoming a better person.

Make no mistake. Developing self discipline will make you a better person. The problem is if you think that this whole things is just not worth doing or it's just more hassle than it's worth, this negative attitude will eventually lead to enough frustration that you will seriously be tempted to quit.

In a May 2005 study conducted by the University of Michigan and published in the journal Cognition and Emotion, 2 experiments features 104 college students. The research subjects were divided into 5 groups.

Each group watched a short film that either created positive emotions or negative emotions or neutral emotions. This group was the control group.

For the other 4 groups, 2 were shown images that triggered a sense of contentment or feelings of joy. The remaining groups were shown images that triggered negative emotions and anger or anxiety. After being shown this stimuli, each participant was given a piece of paper consisting of 20 blank lines.

At the top was the statement "I would like to...". Study participants that were shown images that triggered anger or fear produced the fewest responses. On the other end of the spectrum are the students who were shown images of contentment and joy. They wrote a lot more actions compared to the control group and considerably more than the group shown upsetting images.

The test suggests that if you experienced positive emotions like love, acceptance, contentment, collaboration and joy, you tend to be more optimistic about your life. You tend to see more possibilities.

Step by step guide to practicing self discipline through negativity avoidance.

The first step is to monitor your self talk. If you say things to yourself that undermine or sabotage your ability to get things done or to perform at an optimal level, identify this self talk and try to disrupt it. instead of constantly saying to yourself, "I'm not good looking enough. I'm not smart enough. I don't have the money. I don't have rich parents." on and on it goes, try to mix things up.

Ask yourself questions instead. Instead of always telling yourself, "I don't have money to do that. I can't afford that." say, "How can I afford that? What do I need to do to get something just like that?"

When you ask yourself questions, you trigger your mind's problem solving abilities. You're actually much more resourceful and creative than you give yourself credit for. At the very least, when you ask yourself questions, you open yourself to possibilities of achievement instead of condemning yourself to a certain reality.

Next, monitor your thoughts and clearly see them. Negative people are that way because when they think, they automatically assume that what they're thinking will have a negative conclusion. It's as if negativity was already a forgone conclusion for them.

They only see the worst in situations. They don't want to examine their thoughts for alternative interpretations. If you want to destroy negativity in your life, start with your thoughts.

First, be aware of what you're thinking, then amplify the message that your thoughts are sending. Is there only one way to interpret that thought? Is that thought spot on in terms of the stimuli it uses as evidence?

You'd be surprised as to how many things that go on in your daily life are actually neutral. They're neither here nor there. But unfortunately, due to your negative mental habits, you automatically assume the worst. You read in the very worst conclusion when something more neutral would actually be more appropriate.

By arresting your thoughts and at least second guessing yourself, you put yourself in the habit of arresting a negative thought pattern, eventually, you will get to the point where you can actually think more positively. If you can conclude that your thoughts are not backed up by objective evidence, then you are free to come up with a more positive judgment or interpretation.

Finally, you may want to try hanging out with more positive people. I know, birds of a feather flock together. It's very easy to hang out with negative people. These are people that will tell you in so many ways, based on their words and actions, that you can only go so far and that you're wasting your time if you try to change your situation.

Of course they're not going to tell this to your face. In many cases, they would give you this impression when they talk about themselves. They would say things that normally would insult you if people would say this to your face. But since they're saying it to themselves and you're around to hear them, it's perfectly okay. But guess what happens. They're planting seeds of negativity in your mind.

At some level or other, you're thinking, "Well, if I like these people and this is what they think about themselves or their situation, then this also applies to me. If my friends feels that he is living in a global trap and he's sinking in the quicksand of bad finances, then who am I to judge him. In fact, the things that he talks about and the way he puts things apply to me too."

before you know it, you start absorbing your friend's negativity. This happens all the time. Remember, attitudes are infectious. People don't have to force you to think a certain way.

They don't have to point a gun at your head. Just by being exposed to them and assuming their values, you are allowing yourself to get infected.

Avoid these people. While you're at it, get out of places where you feel stressed or tremendous amount of anxiety. If you notice that you find yourself in certain situations that bring out the worst in you, try to avoid those situations like the plague.

Similarly, if you intend to go on certain websites that anger you or frustrate you, it's probably a good idea to look at other websites. The key here is to reclaim the control you have over your mental and emotional state.

You have a lot more control than you give yourself credit for. Remember, you have to watch what you feed your head. When everything you watch is negative, corrosive, destructive and pessimistic, don't be surprised if you become what you watch. Pay close attention to the media that you choose to devour every single day.

Chapter 10: Harness the Power of Beliefs To Keep You Moving

Why did I put belief at the end of this process? You might be thinking that the most logical part to believe is the beginning. Well, based on experience, this is the proper place for belief. How come?

Belief that turns into an immovable mental fortress quickly feeds off the "cement" of lived experience. In other words, if you believe that you are self disciplined enough to handle a lot of life's challenges, you are more likely to act on that belief if you have reason to.

These reasons are not emotional and mental in nature. Those reasons are not good enough because if those are your only reasons, you're basically just trying to psyche yourself up. You're trying to hypnotize yourself into thinking you are a certain way when your physical reality highlights the fact that you are nothing but the complete opposite.

Do you see the disconnect? Do you see why it's a bad idea to put belief first when it comes to self discipline? Reserve it for the last stage. How come? By this point, you have tried self discipline. You have exercised it day after day. You have fine tuned your willpower.

By this point, you should have something to show for all your efforts. This is called objective evidence. Now, of course, just like anything else in life, there are always 2 sides to the story. You can choose to look a these objective evidence in a completely optimistic way or you can take the other side.

But the good news is there is at least objective evidence. You are able to do it. Nobody can take this away from you. Nobody can say to you that this is all in your head, that you're just playing games with your head. This is real because you can point to those objective things you did and the outcomes that you produced.

The key here is to believe that you can be self disciplined by looking at your outcomes as proof. This enables you to foster a self sustaining belief that scales up over time. The more you believe that you can be self disciplined, the more you're likely to act. The more stress you put on self discipline, the stronger it becomes.

You're able to put up with a lot more things. You're able to become more patient. You're able to deal with more challenges. But this belief is built on the bed rock of actual lived experience. There are actual examples of your self discipline. You're not just engaged in wishful thinking. You're not just looking out and hoping and wishing that somehow, someway, you'll be more self disciplined.

Instead, you're looking at your actual outcomes. When you base your belief in this, your belief acts like gasoline poured on burning embers of hope. Don't be surprised if you have a raging fire in front of you that burns bright with hope, possibility and eagerness.

This is what you need to get an upward spiral going. The more you believe in your ability to practice self discipline, the more likely you are to take action and the more likely you are to get the results that you're looking for. This, in turn, triggers even more belief, you feel better about yourself, you estimate your capabilities more highly, you become more confident, you feel more competent and on and on it goes .

Compare this with what you have right now. What you have right now is a vague plan. A wish. The secret to self discipline is consistent focus and this is not going to happen unless you build a super structure of belief on top of it that will sustain you through the tough times and there will be a lot of tough times ahead.

It's Time to Take Action!

Building self discipline can help you in all areas of your life. The great thing about self discipline is it's a personal trait that you can work on wherever you are at whatever time. Regardless of the situation you find yourself in, there is always an opportunity to practice self discipline.

In fact, if you have certain negative memories, maybe memories of abuse, betrayal or humiliation, you can practice self discipline just by how you respond to those memories. Are you going to continuously react the way you normally do? Are you going to get upset? Are you going to get thrown off track? Or are you going to respond based on your values?

Are you going to take ownership of your negative emotions and let them go? It's very easy to think that self discipline can only take place in certain situations. Stop fooling yourself. Self discipline is one thing that you can exercise pretty much around the clock regardless of your physical location.

The good news is the tips that I've outlined in this book will give you the framework that you need to build a high enough level of self discipline so you can put in the work, time and focus you need to get where you want to go.

Maybe you want to become a better artist. Maybe you want to become a more insightful creator. Maybe you want to earn more money or you desire more respect for your work. Whatever your goals may be, self discipline is the key.

If you can not master yourself, the world will master you. I know that sounds stark and at some levels, it may seem harsh, but it's also the truth. I wish you nothing but success and power in your life.

The author makes no representations or warranties with respect to the accuracy or completeness of the contents of this work and specifically disclaims all warranties, including without limitation warranties of fitness for a particular purpose. No warranty may be created or extended by sales or promotional materials. The advice and recipes contained herein may not be suitable for everyone. This work is sold with the understanding that the author is not engaged in rendering medical, legal or other professional advice or services. If professional assistance is required, the services of a competent professional person should be sought. The author shall not be liable for damages arising here from. The fact that an individual, organization of website is referred to in this work as a citation and/or potential source of further information does not mean that the author endorses the information the individual, organization to website may provide or recommendations they/it may make. Further, readers should be aware that Internet websites listed in this work might have changed or disappeared between when this work was written and when it is read.

Adherence to all applicable laws and regulations, including international, federal, state, and local governing professional licensing, business practices, advertising, and all other aspects of doing business in any jurisdiction in the world is the sole responsibility of the purchaser or reader.

Made in the USA
Middletown, DE
25 March 2019